I0429777

CHRIS E. HOMES

A Guide to Hiring a Great Property Manager

Discover the Best Questions to Ask Before Hiring a Property Manager

Copyright © 2024 by Chris E. Homes

All rights reserved. No part of this publication may be reproduced, stored or transmitted in any form or by any means, electronic, mechanical, photocopying, recording, scanning, or otherwise without written permission from the publisher. It is illegal to copy this book, post it to a website, or distribute it by any other means without permission.

Chris E. Homes has no responsibility for the persistence or accuracy of URLs for external or third-party Internet Websites referred to in this publication and does not guarantee that any content on such Websites is, or will remain, accurate or appropriate.

Designations used by companies to distinguish their products are often claimed as trademarks. All brand names and product names used in this book and on its cover are trade names, service marks, trademarks and registered trademarks of their respective owners. The publishers and the book are not associated with any product or vendor mentioned in this book. None of the companies referenced within the book have endorsed the book.

First edition

This book was professionally typeset on Reedsy.
Find out more at reedsy.com

Contents

A Guide to Hiring a Great Property Manager   1

The Essential Role of a Great Property Manager   3

The Pitfalls of Opting for the Cheapest Option   7

Overlooked Considerations in the Hiring Process   12

Insurance   15

Repairs   17

Management Fees   20

Preventative Maintenance and Inspections   24

Tenant Screening, Compliance & Funds Management   28

Leases and Evictions   31

Software Systems and Marketing   34

Pets, ESA, and Service Animals   38

The Onboarding Process   40

What Does Rent Ready Mean?   46

Size Isn't Everything   52

Making the Final Decision   56

Conclusion: Hiring a Great Property Manager   59

Resources   60

A Guide to Hiring a Great Property Manager

Discover the Best Questions to Ask Before Hiring a Property Manager

Welcome to "A Guide to Hiring a Great Property Manager" – your straightforward resource for asking the right questions when selecting a property manager. Designed for both new landlords and investors, this book equips you with essential knowledge for making informed decisions when selecting a property management company. This isn't just a compilation of generic advice; it's a thoughtfully curated collection of insider tips from an experienced property manager.

What sets this book apart is its vision – to empower you with the right questions. Hiring a property manager is not a one-size-fits-all endeavor; it's about understanding the specific needs of your property and ensuring a harmonious partnership with the management company.

If you're a new landlord or investor navigating the complexities of property management, this guide is custom-made for you. It's crafted for those who cherish their assets, aim to minimize liability, and seek the advantages of professional property management services. This isn't for slumlords or penny-pinching owners; it's for individuals dedicated to optimizing the performance and well-being of their real estate investments.

As we embark on this journey together, it's crucial to recognize the important role of a property manager. Beyond administrative tasks, they serve as your shield against legal troubles, your guide through Fair Housing Laws, and the assurance of a well-maintained investment. Discover not only our integral role in the process but also the essential features, benefits, and value that come with exceptional professional property management services.

Discover the secrets of hiring an outstanding property manager as we share the importance of formulating relevant questions during the interview process, empowering you to navigate your responsibilities with confidence and competence.

The Essential Role of a Great Property Manager

"**A** Great Property Manager is Key to Success in Real Estate"

In the world of real estate wealth creation, one often underestimates a crucial player - the property manager. This chapter unravels the significance of an exceptional property manager, exploring why their role is paramount in safeguarding assets, reducing liability, and securing long-term benefits. As Robert Kiyosaki said, "A great property manager is key to success in real estate".

Securing Assets: The Foundation of Prosperity

To fully comprehend the impact of property management, it's essential to grasp the essence of real estate as an investment. Properties aren't merely structures; they are valuable assets capable of generating income and appreciating over time. Entrusting these assets to a capable manager ensures a smooth journey and shields against potential storms.

The choice of a property manager transcends mere financial considerations; it is a strategic decision to safeguard and enhance the performance of your assets. In the pursuit of wealth creation, prioritizing quality over cost in the hiring process becomes a fundamental principle.

Quality Over Cost: Investing in Excellence

In the world of property management, cutting corners can be a costly endeavor. Opting for a subpar property manager to save a few dollars may seem like a prudent move initially, but the long-term consequences can be detrimental. A great property manager operates as a guardian of your investment, navigating challenges, and maximizing returns.

The hiring process should be viewed through the lens of asset protection and value enhancement. Remember, the true cost of a poor property manager is not just measured in fees but in potential income loss, property damage, and legal liabilities.

Legal and Ethical Considerations: Navigating the Landscape

Understanding the legal and ethical aspects of property management is vital for navigating the complexities of real estate. In this section, we explore what property managers need to handle to ensure compliance and ethical practices.

The legal landscape is characterized by an array of federal, state, and local laws that govern various facets of property management. From tenant rights to landlord responsibilities, a competent property manager must possess a comprehensive understanding of these regulations. This extends to Fair Housing Laws, which mandate equal treatment for all individuals in housing transactions, preventing discrimination based on factors such as race, gender, religion, or disability.

Property management is fraught with legal and ethical considerations. Understanding and abiding by Fair Housing Laws at federal, state, and local levels is not just a compliance requirement; it is a moral and professional obligation for both the owner and property manager.

Essentially, opting for a property manager proficient in Fair Housing laws is a strategic investment in risk mitigation, aiming to steer clear of legal issues. This proactive measure not only safeguards you and your assets but also ensures the promotion of fairness and equality in housing practices.

NARPM: Elevating Standards in Property Management

Welcome to the forefront of property management excellence - the National Association of Residential Property Managers (NARPM). NARPM is not just an association; it's the forefront of professionalism in property management.

Being a NARPM member signifies a commitment to a higher duty of care as a housing provider. It's a declaration to adhere to elevated standards, safeguarding that your property is managed by someone who comprehends the nuances of the industry and is dedicated to excellence.

Hiring a property manager affiliated with NARPM is strongly recommended for several reasons. NARPM members go beyond ordinary standards, committing to a level of professionalism that ensures your property is handled with precision and expertise. By choosing a NARPM-affiliated property manager, you're opting for top-tier professionalism, industry knowledge, and a dedication to the highest standards of property management.

The Power of a Great Property Manager

In conclusion, the significance of a great property manager is critical.

This chapter has highlighted their key role in safeguarding assets, prioritizing quality, and adhering to legal and ethical standards. An exceptional property manager goes beyond routine tasks, becoming a strategic partner in ensuring your property thrives and remains compliant with regulations. As you venture into property ownership, choosing a great property manager is fundamental for enduring success and optimal asset performance.

The Pitfalls of Opting for the Cheapest Option

I n the intricate dance of property management, the allure of the lowest price can be a treacherous waltz. As we navigate, it is paramount to heed the cautionary tale against making decisions solely based on the monthly rate, the cheapest option may cost you more in the long run.

The Illusion of Savings

When the siren song of a bargain beckons, it's tempting to succumb to the allure of the cheapest property management company. After all, who doesn't relish the idea of saving a few dollars each month? However, true wealth is not found in counting pennies but in strategic decisions that foster long-term prosperity.

Choosing the cheapest property management company may appear as a financial victory initially, but the risks lurking beneath the surface can quickly erode any perceived savings. It's essential to recognize that the monthly rate is but one facet of the broader picture.

The Cost of Being a Cheapskate

Opting for the cheapest property management option isn't merely a financial decision; it's a strategic move that can impact property value, tenant satisfaction, and the overall success of your property management venture. Being a cheapskate often leads to a diminishing return on investment.

Property Value Deterioration

Property value is intricately tied to its condition and management. Choosing the cheapest option might mean cutting corners on essential maintenance and upkeep, leading to a decline in property value over time.

Tenant Satisfaction and Retention

Happy tenants are the lifeblood of successful property management. Opting for the cheapest management company may result in inadequate tenant services, leading to dissatisfaction and turnover. Landlords and investors should be aware that a continual turnover of tenants can prove to be more financially burdensome than opting for quality property management right from the beginning.

Beyond Rent Collection: The Unseen Responsibilities

Property management transcends the mere routine of rent collection, revealing an intricate tapestry of responsibilities concealed beneath the surface. These unseen obligations wield a profound impact on the overall prosperity and well-being of real estate investments.

The scope of property management responsibilities is extensive, involving a diverse array of tasks. From marketing and advertising to thorough tenant screening, meticulous property inspections, developing and implementing preventive maintenance schedules, precision in scheduling and tracking repair work orders, emergency service calls, lease management, lease renewals, lease addendums, coordination with vendors, building relationships with service providers, managing utility coordination, and executing precise accounting procedures, are all essential components. Additionally, responsibilities include ensuring the proper handling of owner and tenant funds, meticulous statement preparations, addressing tenant concerns promptly, delivering comprehensive end-of-year reporting, rent ready processes, security deposit disbursements, rent distributions, continuous professional education, fraud avoidance, strict adherence to Privacy laws, Fair Housing laws, and compliance with state and local regulations, diligent communication with owners and tenants, developing property profiles, verification of renters' insurance, and the establishment of tenant and owner portals for streamlined access and document management, all adds further layers to the intricate and multifaceted nature inherent in proficient property management. All of this and more, with a continuous 24/7 on-call commitment, emphasizing the comprehensive approach required for success in this field. It's not simply collecting rent!

Furthermore, property managers bear the weight of fostering positive relationships with tenants, surpassing the realm of rent collection. It involves effective communication, adept conflict resolution, and ensuring tenant satisfaction. Neglecting these relational aspects can lead to tenant dissatisfaction, contributing to increased turnover and potential vacancies that directly impact the property's revenue stream.

The unseen responsibilities of property managers require an intricate organization of various tasks to ensure the seamless operation and prosperity of real estate investments.owners and investors need to discern that the perceived cost-cutting associated with choosing the cheapest management option often translates into an insufficient handling of these responsibilities. In essence, comprehending and appreciating these numerous unseen responsibilities is indispensable for making informed decisions that contribute to the enduring success of property management.

Legal Compliance and Risk Mitigation

Property managers bear the weight of legal responsibilities, from navigating complex tenant-landlord laws to ensuring compliance with Fair Housing regulations. Cutting costs and hiring the wrong property manager can lead to legal troubles that far outweigh the perceived savings.

One of the primary unseen responsibilities involves legal compliance and risk mitigation. Property managers navigate the intricate landscape of tenant-landlord laws, ensuring adherence to legal regulations and compliance. Mistakes, intentional or accidental, can expose owners and investors to unnecessary risks, leading to potential legal troubles that may far surpass any perceived savings from choosing a budget-friendly management option.

Stress and Burnout in Property Management

Engaging in property management can be inherently stressful. Opting for the cheapest option may initially seem appealing, but it often results in compromised management quality, leading to elevated stress levels for both property owners and property managers. It is essential to acknowledge that investing in quality management is a strategic move, reducing stress and contributing to long-term success. In the intricate orchestration of property management, it's vital to resist the allure of the cheapest option and prioritize enduring quality for sustained prosperity.

Overlooked Considerations in the Hiring Process

I n the pursuit of securing a reliable property manager, it's imperative to consider the often-overlooked steps of the hiring process. This chapter aims to equip new owners, existing landlords, and investors with a comprehensive understanding of the key considerations that go beyond the surface. As we navigate through this crucial phase, the focus will be on researching potential property managers, scrutinizing credentials, and preparing a list of questions to ask.

Researching Potential Property Managers

The journey to hiring a great property manager commences with thorough research. It involves diving into their reputation and track record. This includes scrutinizing online reviews, seeking recommendations from local real estate networks, and investigating their performance with other property owners. A reputable property manager will gladly provide references, offering valuable insights into their professionalism and performance.

The research of their website and current listings unveils an additional layer of valuable insights. A meticulously maintained website stands as a testament to professionalism, while the examination of current or past listings serves as a window into the manager's competence in effective property marketing.

The evaluation of current listings extends beyond a cursory examination; it manifests as a tangible demonstration of their marketing approach. Scrutinize whether their listings boast professional-grade photography and articulate, well-crafted property descriptions. This review offers a glimpse into how they would strategically market your property.

A well-curated website and compelling property listings are not just aesthetic components but reflections of an adept and effective property management strategy, let these facets guide your assessment, ensuring that the chosen professional aligns with your property management aspirations.

Checking Credentials

Credentials serve as a tangible demonstration of a property manager's expertise and commitment to professionalism. In this section, we emphasize the paramount importance of verifying credentials, such as certifications and memberships from reputable organizations and affiliations with recognized industry associations like the National Association of Residential Property Managers (NARPM).

"Professional Members of NARPM® are individuals who must be engaged in the management of residential properties as agents for others. They are licensed in those states that require licensing. Or are employees of a company, or property owner, who handles all aspects of the residential property management. These individuals must comply with real estate license law for their state but do not have to hold a license. Professional Members have also completed current NARPM® Code of Ethics training"

When considering a property manager, it's crucial to hire an industry expert dedicated to the role, avoiding individuals experimenting or working part-time in property management, such as realtors seeking to diversify their activities. This focused approach ensures reliability and expertise in marketing your property effectively.

Insurance

Asking the Right Questions and Why

When seeking a property manager, the art of asking targeted questions becomes your compass in navigating the diverse landscape of property management. This series of chapters provides insider tips from an experienced property manager, steering you beyond generic internet inquiries. The focus is on the value of precision in questioning, focusing on key categories of services, experience, and communication.

As you embark on this journey, the chapters are designed to categorize inquiries into crucial aspects of property management. From insurance to maintenance, legal compliance to tenant screening, each question is meticulously crafted to unveil insights that go beyond surface-level considerations. The goal is not just to gather answers but to ensure your decision is well-informed and tailored to your specific needs.

Insurance

Adequate insurance is not just a formality but a fundamental layer of protection for both your property and the property management company, establishing a safety net in unforeseen circumstances.

When inquiring about the insurance held by the property management company, it's crucial to ensure they possess comprehensive coverage. Look for a company equipped with general liability insurance, which protects against property damage and injuries. Additionally, an errors and omissions (E&O) policy is essential; it covers professional mistakes that might occur during the course of managing your property.

Q. Ask the P.M. What type of insurance coverage do you have?

The only answer when hiring a great property manager should be that they have both General Liability and Errors and Omissions Coverage!

Insider Tip: Safeguarding your assets is paramount as a property owner. We strongly advise you to secure ample coverage with a one-million-dollar liability plan and an umbrella insurance policy for an added layer of protection for each investment property. Also, take the proactive step of including the property manager you hire as an "ADDITIONAL INSURED" on your Rental Homeowners Insurance policy for liability purposes. This isn't an area to skimp on; always prioritize minimizing liability and exposure to fortify your financial protection.

Repairs

B y posing these questions and considering the provided advice, property owners can make informed decisions, ensuring that the property management company's approach to repairs aligns with their expectations for tenant satisfaction and efficient property maintenance.

Q. How do tenants submit a repair request?

Insider Tip: Ensure that the property management company provides a user-friendly and accessible system for tenants to submit repair requests. This may involve online portals, mobile apps, or dedicated communication channels. A streamlined process encourages prompt reporting.

Q. How long does it take to reply to tenants?

Insider Tip: Ideally, tenants should receive acknowledgment within 24 hours. Inquire about clear communication protocols or automated responses that manage tenant expectations and offer timely updates on repair progress.

Q. How do you manage repair request tickets?

Insider Tip: Inquire about the property management company's method for organizing and prioritizing repair request tickets. A well-organized system is crucial for efficiently tracking and addressing repairs. Look for companies that use technology or software to streamline this process.

Q. How do tenants report emergencies after normal business hours?

Insider Tip: Discuss if there is an emergency reporting system for tenants outside regular business hours. It should be clear, accessible, and capable of handling urgent matters promptly.

Q. How do you bill for repairs, and do you charge any additional fees for scheduling and coordinating?

When discussing repair-related fees, inquire about the property management company's billing structure. Some companies may charge owner fees for scheduling and coordinating repairs.

When comparing monthly management fees, it's essential to factor in how repairs are handled and if any additional repair fees apply. For instance, a company with a lower 7% monthly management fee might tack on 10%-15% more on every repair invoice. On the other hand, a company with a higher 10% monthly fee may not have additional charges for repairs. The latter might offer better value, considering that these services are included without extra fees.

Insider Tip: Selecting a property manager based solely on the monthly fee is a common mistake. A comprehensive assessment of monthly fees, additional services, and overall value is crucial when making this decision.

Management Fees

I n the space of property management, the Management Fee serves as the monthly charge applied by your property manager for their services. This fee structure may manifest as a flat rate or a percentage of the monthly rents, offering different approaches depending on the property management company.

Some companies follow a full-service plan, encompassing all aspects of property management, while others adopt tiered pricing models, presenting varying service levels at different price points.

When scrutinizing and comparing management fees, it's imperative to dive into the details, understanding the services encompassed in the fee and identifying any potential additional charges that may arise during the course of management but aren't explicitly covered in the monthly fee. Relying solely on the monthly fee for selecting a property manager can result in oversights.

Q. Can you explain and itemize your management fees?

Insider Tip: Request a detailed breakdown of the management fees. Understand the components and services covered by the fee to gauge the overall value offered by the property management company.

Q. Do you charge a flat rate or a percentage of monthly rent?

Insider Tip: Clarify the fee structure employed by the property management company. Whether it's a flat rate or a percentage of monthly rent, this information is pivotal for evaluating the financial implications of the agreement.

Q. How am I billed if the tenant is not paying rent, is it based on rent rue or rents collected?

Insider Tip: Investigate the billing process during non-payment scenarios. Understand if the management fee is based on "Rent Due" or "Rents Collected." This insight provides clarity on the financial aspects during tenant-related challenges.

By posing these questions and considering the provided tips, property owners can navigate the intricacies of management fees, ensuring transparency and alignment with their financial expectations in the property management partnership.

Terms

- Percentage of Rent: Property managers collect a percentage of the monthly rent as the property management fee.
- Flat fee: A specific dollar amount paid to the property manager each month.

Rent Due vs. Rent Collected

- Rents Due: If based on "Rent Due," the property manager will collect money from you even if the tenants are not paying rent.
- Rents Collected: If based on "Rent Collected," the property manager would collect money from ONLY if the tenant paid rent; it's based on rent received. However, they might still have a minimum fee to cover their expenses.

Other Fees

Many management companies implement specific fees for services like lease renewals, tenant placements, and new onboarding. Inquiring about other fees provides a general view of the costs involved in initiating a partnership. Armed with this knowledge, you can make informed decisions that align with your financial expectations and overall property management strategy.

Renewal Fee

Q. What is your lease renewal fee?

Insider Tip: Property management companies impose a Renewal Fee when existing leases are extended. Understanding this fee structure ensures you are prepared for potential costs associated with lease renewals.

New Tenant Placement Fee

Q. What is your new tenant placement fee?

Insider Tip: When a new tenant is introduced to your property, certain management companies charge a placement fee. Clarifying this upfront avoids surprises and allows you to factor in costs associated with securing new tenants.

Onboarding/Setup Fee

Q. Do you implement an onboarding or setup fee for new clients?

Insider Tip: It's common for property management companies to charge an initial fee when onboarding new clients and properties.

Understanding and addressing these fees ensures transparency in your property management agreement.

Preventative Maintenance and Inspections

P**reventative Maintenance**

Prioritizing preventive maintenance is essential for your property's longevity. Understanding the property manager's approach helps assess their commitment to proactive measures, preventing potential issues. This ensures not only the property's well-being but also enhances tenant satisfaction. A reliable property manager conducts routine inspections, addressing issues promptly and maintaining all systems in optimal condition. Additionally, they develop a recommended maintenance plan to safeguard your investment.

Q. What strategies do you employ for preventive maintenance?

Insider Tip: When posing this question, the property manager should be able to clearly relay how they handle maintenance and communicate these strategies to property owners. It should cover a comprehensive annual schedule addressing all major systems. This includes but is not limited to HVAC systems, plumbing, electrical systems, roofing, and structural elements.

Preventive maintenance encompasses routine checks, cleaning, and minor repairs ensures that the property remains in optimal condition.

Property owners benefit from a property manager who recognizes the proactive nature of preventive maintenance and includes it as a fundamental aspect of their management strategy.

Inspections

Regular inspections are paramount for maintaining property standards, serving as a cornerstone in proactive property management. It's crucial to comprehend the various types, their quality, and the frequency of inspections to ensure they align with your expectations. The quality of reports and the software used is crucial in differentiating between mediocre and top-notch property management companies. Varying structures and fees exist among companies.

Q. What types of inspections do you conduct, and how often?

Insider Tip: This question aims to reveal the diversity and frequency of inspections, ensuring a proactive approach to property management. Ask for a sample report to review.

Q. What software do you use to conduct these inspections?

Insider Tip: The response to this question unveils the sophistication and efficiency of the property management company's inspection process. In today's digital age, a property manager equipped with specialized software demonstrates a commitment to modern, streamlined practices. Property owners should view the absence of inspection software as a potential red flag.

Q. Do the inspections include pictures, how many are taken?

Insider Tip: This question delves into the depth and clarity of the inspection reports, ensuring comprehensive documentation.

Q. Are the inspections delivered in a report form?

Insider Tip: Knowing if the inspections are compiled into a structured report helps assess the accessibility and professionalism of the documentation.

Q. Are inspections available in my owner portal?

Insider Tip: This inquiry focuses on the convenience and transparency of accessing inspection reports through an owner portal, enhancing your involvement in the property management process.

Examples of Common Reports Performed by Property Management Companies:

- *Move-In Inspections*
- *Move-Out Inspections*
- *Preventative Maintenance Inspections*
- *Lease Renewal Inspections*
- *Drive-By Inspections*
- *Inspections to track repairs and damages*

Advice: Choose a property management company that employs robust software such as zInspector or an equivalent. This comprehensive tool not only protects your property but also meticulously documents conditions during repairs, move-ins, and move-outs. With automatic timestamps, user-stamps, and GPS stamps on pictures, it produces detailed reports, making it one of the industry's best. This choice ensures accountability, benefiting both tenants and owners, safeguarding their interests.

Insider Tip: Effective documentation through pictures and videos facilitates easy comparisons, reducing potential legal issues tenants may pursue over a security deposit during move-out. This meticulous approach ensures a transparent and smooth process, contributing to a positive property management experience.

Tenant Screening, Compliance & Funds Management

Tenant Screening

Tenant screening is a crucial determinant of securing reliable and responsible tenants for your property. When selecting a property manager, prioritize those with a transparent and compliant screening process that upholds fair treatment and consistent standards. Inquire about their specific criteria, ensuring it aligns with your preferences and understanding how they enforce these standards.

The tenant screening process typically involves a comprehensive evaluation of applicants based on factors such as credit history, rental history, income verification, and criminal background checks. Engaging in a detailed conversation with the property management company helps property owners understand their screening criteria.

Q. What criteria do you use for tenant screening?

Insider Tip: Opt for property managers who embrace an online platform for tenant applications, promoting accessibility and streamlining the application process for all parties involved.

Legal Knowledge and Compliance

Property owners are encouraged to scrutinize potential property management companies on their approach to staying abreast of landlord-tenant laws ensuring compliance.The response to this question unveils the property manager's commitment to legal compliance. In an ever-evolving legal landscape, property owners need assurance that their chosen property management company is well-versed in the intricacies of landlord-tenant laws.

Q. How do you stay updated on landlord-tenant laws, and how do you ensure compliance?

Insider Tip: A responsible and informed property manager prioritizes continuous education. Look for those who engage in ongoing training, attend industry seminars, and actively participate in professional organizations.

Furthermore, inquire about their internal processes and protocols to ensure compliance with the latest legal requirements. This commitment not only safeguards property owners from legal pitfalls but also reflects the property manager's dedication to responsible and ethical property management practices.

Handling of Funds

When entrusting a property management company with the financial aspects of your investment, property owners should seek explicit details on how tenant security deposit funds and rental funds are managed.

Trust Account Management

In addition to the handling of funds, property owners should inquire specifically about trust account management. A property management company should maintain a trust account for security deposits, demonstrating a commitment to safeguarding these funds. Property owners should seek assurance that trust accounts are managed ethically, with proper record-keeping and adherence to legal and industry standards.

Q. How are tenant security deposit funds and rental funds handled?

Insider Tip: Property owners should inquire about the segregation of tenant security deposit funds and owner funds in dedicated accounts, ensuring strict adherence to legal requirements.

It's imperative that these practices not only align with industry standards but also adhere to legal requirements.

Leases and Evictions

Lease Agreements

Lease agreements are the foundation of the landlord-tenant relationship, outlining the terms that govern the property. It's crucial to delve into the specifics of how lease agreements are managed, with a focus on the language used.

Q. How is your lease written and was it attorney reviewed?

Insider Tip: Attorney reviewed leases signify a commitment to legal soundness and thorough understanding of applicable regulations. A well-crafted lease, especially when attorney-reviewed, is a crucial tool that holds significance in potential litigation scenarios. We recommend requesting to read and review a sample lease.

Q. Do you include additional addendums with your lease and what kind?

Insider Tip: Many property managers include specific addendums to address unique aspects of the property or circumstances. Understanding the types of addendums used can provide insights into how thoroughly potential issues are addressed.

Q. Have you been sued, and did you prevail?

Insider Tip: A history of legal challenges may indicate potential shortcomings in the property manager's practices. Understanding how they navigated legal issues and whether they prevailed offers valuable context.

A well-written lease agreement is not just a formality; it is a foundational document that defines the relationship between landlords and tenants. In the event of disputes or legal challenges, the lease agreement serves as a critical tool for resolution. Property owners should prioritize property managers who understand the importance of crafting comprehensive and legally sound leases, as it significantly contributes to a smooth and legally defensible landlord-tenant relationship.

Lease Enforcement

Lease enforcement is pivotal for maintaining property standards and ensuring tenant compliance. Understanding the property manager's approach to addressing lease violations is crucial for a well-managed property.

Q. How do you handle lease violations and enforce lease terms?

Insider Tip: A proactive approach to lease enforcement involves clear procedures, timely communication, and fair but firm actions. Property managers with well-established enforcement strategies are better equipped to maintain a property that adheres to standards.

Q. Once the rent is considered late, what is your next step?

Insider Tip: Prompt action in response to late rent is essential. Property managers should have clear protocols for communication, late fees, and any subsequent steps. A well-defined process ensures consistency and helps avoid potential conflicts with tenants.

Q. How many days in the grace period?

Insider Tip: It's essential to inquire about the property manager's next steps once a tenant is late beyond the grace period, usually ranging from 3-5 days; ensuring you understand their procedures for handling late payments and outlines the subsequent steps.

Evictions

Evictions are complex and challenging scenarios that necessitate a strategic approach. Discussing the property manager's strategy for handling evictions provides assurance in navigating difficult circumstances while adhering to legal requirements.

Q. What is your approach to handling evictions?

Insider Tip: An experienced property manager should have a well-defined and legally compliant eviction strategy, an outline of associated costs and time frames. Understanding their approach offers peace of mind and confidence in their ability to handle challenging situations effectively.

Software Systems and Marketing

P**roperty Management Software Systems**

In the contemporary landscape of property management, technology stands as a cornerstone for operational excellence. The adeptness with which a property manager employs software and systems provides valuable insights into their efficiency, communication practices, and overall modernization of property management tasks.

Key Features to Inquire About:

- **Tenant Portal:** An accessible platform for tenants, facilitating seamless communication and efficient handling of repair requests.
- **Owner Portal:** A dedicated space for owners, ensuring transparency in financial transactions, access to comprehensive reports, and statements.
- **Online Rent Payment Links:** Convenient avenues for online rent payments, enhancing the experience for both tenants and owners.
- **24/7 Accessibility:** Confirm the availability of these features for uninterrupted access around the clock.

Q. What property management software systems do you use?

The key is ensuring your property manager uses professional management software. The specific type matters less than having the right tools for effective and customized property management.

Insider Tip: By discussing the property manager's use of software and systems, you gain insights into their tech-savviness. This ensures streamlined operations, effective communication, and overall improved efficiency in property management.

Marketing and Photography

Effective marketing is crucial for attracting high-quality tenants. Discussing the property manager's marketing strategies, particularly the use of professional photography and video, provides insights into their ability to showcase properties effectively. This not only improves tenant attraction but also ensures maximum exposure for your property in the rental market.

Q. How do you market rental properties?

Insider Tip: When discussing marketing strategies, inquire about syndication – the process of listing properties on various platforms. Ask the property manager about the specific websites and platforms they utilize to maximize exposure.

Additionally, discuss their measures to prevent falling victim to fraud, particularly in the context of predatory listings scams.

Q. Do you employ professional photography?

Insider Tip: Great photography and video are essential to getting your property rented quickly! Tech-savvy tenants screen properties using the internet and social media, they expect access to amazing pictures.

Self-Showing Technology for Rental Properties

The use of self-tour software is a controversial topic in the property management industry, particularly in the context of showing rental properties. This technology has transformed the traditional approach to property tours, offering prospective tenants more flexibility and convenience. However, property managers and owners need to weigh the pros and cons carefully.

Pros of Self-Tours:

1. Convenience: Prospective tenants can view properties at their convenience without relying on a scheduled appointment.
2. Efficiency: Self-tours may speed up the leasing process, allowing more prospective tenants to view the property in a shorter time frame.

Cons of Self-Tours:

1. Safety Concerns: Allowing strangers to enter vacant properties without supervision raises security and safety concerns. There's uncertainty about how well prospective renters will treat the property and whether they'll follow proper security measures.
2. Utility Costs: There is a risk of prospective tenants leaving lights, HVAC, or other utilities running after a self-tour, resulting in additional costs for property owners.

Q. Do you use self touring technology for showings?

Insider Tip: When considering the use of self-tour software, property owners should carefully evaluate the pros and cons. While it offers convenience and potential efficiency, the safety and security aspects should be a primary consideration. Property managers can provide guidance, but ultimately, property owners should decide what aligns best with their preferences and risk tolerance.

Pets, ESA, and Service Animals

When conversing with a property manager, ensure you discuss pet policies, emotional support animals and service animals. Individuals with disabilities may rely on service animals and emotional support animals (ESAs) for various reasons. According to HUD, an assistance animal is one that works, provides assistance, or performs tasks for a person with a disability. Additionally, it can offer emotional support that alleviates the effects of a person's disability. Importantly, these animals are not considered pets.

Q. How do you handle applicants with an ESA or service animal?

Legal Responsibilities: Landlords must adhere to laws governing ESAs and service animals. They are not subject to pet policies and should be accommodated within the guidelines of reasonable accommodation laws. It is crucial for property managers and landlords to be aware of and compliant with these regulations.

Insider Tip: When selecting a property manager, it is highly recommended to choose one that utilizes screening processes like PetScreening.com. which was developed by property managers for property managers.

PetScreening.com is a simple, robust, and secure solution for reviewing reasonable accommodation requests related to service animals and support animals. The platform manages accommodation request reviews, providing property managers with an efficient tool to handle such requests and effectively manage their assets. This ensures compliance with legal obligations and reduces your liability.

Q. Do you charge pet fees or pet rent, and how are they determined?

Insider Tip: Explore the advantages and disadvantages of allowing pets. Opting for a strict no-pet policy might result in fewer potential tenants and a prolonged search for renters. Conversely, being open to pets can enhance your property's appeal and generate additional income through increased pet rent. Remember, ESA and Service Animals are not subject to pet policies.

The Onboarding Process

Welcome to a comprehensive exploration of the onboarding process designed to empower you with the insights and knowledge needed to embark on a successful partnership with your property management company. In this chapter, we'll unravel the details of getting started, covering everything from the fundamental steps in onboarding to understanding essential standard forms. We'll also dive into the critical concept of a "Rent Ready Home" and emphasize the significance of the Property Management Agreement.

By the end of this chapter, you'll not only be well-versed in the onboarding process but also feel equipped with the knowledge to actively participate in creating a successful partnership with your property management company.

Onboarding Process

Initiating the onboarding process is a crucial step in laying the groundwork for a successful partnership with your property management company. Throughout this phase, we will thoroughly explore the fundamental steps and requirements, prioritizing transparent communication to ensure a smooth transition. It's essential to note that each property management company may have its distinct onboarding procedures, and this section aims to provide you with practical insights to navigate through this vital initiation phase smoothly.

What to Expect: A Glimpse into the Onboarding Journey

Documentation Overview

This section provides an in-depth look at the fundamental forms and processes you can expect when hiring a great property manager, including brief descriptions of their purposes. These documents pave the way for clear communication and ensure efficient operational procedures for a well-managed property.

Property Evaluation:

The property manager must initiate a comprehensive preliminary inspection of the subject property, a crucial and informative step. This evaluation is essential for gauging the current condition of the property, providing recommendations, and estimating the anticipated costs required to transition it into a "Rent Ready" state.

Rental Market Analysis:

We recommend requesting a recent Rental Market Analysis for your property; property managers typically provide this service at no cost. This involves a thorough examination of recent rental listings in the neighboring areas. By factoring in elements such as location, size, and the condition of your home, this analysis provides a reliable estimate of the monthly rental market rate for your property.

Property Management Agreement:

The Property Management Agreement serves as the official contract between the property owner and the manager. This legally binding document outlines the procedures, policies, and fees that govern the business relationship. It is imperative to read this document carefully before signing. If any part of the agreement is unclear or not agreed upon, signing should only occur after addressing and resolving any questions.

Expectations:

This component clearly lays out the obligations and responsibilities of both the property owner and the property manager. The purpose is to eliminate any potential for misplaced expectations, ensuring that both parties fully understand and acknowledge their respective roles.

Reserves:

As part of your agreement, you will need to maintain funds on deposit with the property manager, known as reserves. These reserves are specifically designated for covering repairs and addressing small incidentals that may arise during the course of property management. The reserve amount varies based on factors such as your home's size, condition, and the property management minimums. Typically, reserves range from $250 to $500 for an average home. Keep in mind that there is no set amount, and you can expect this number to differ for each property manager.

Owner's Handbook:

The Owner's Handbook, acting as a dynamic supplement to the Management Agreement, serves as an expansive guide to understanding the intricacies of the property management agreement. Though not universally adopted by all property managers, it stands as an invaluable tool for both the property manager and the owner. This comprehensive resource delves into the finer details, offering clarity and insights beyond what the Management Agreement may cover.

Intake Forms:

Owner and Property Intake Forms serve as indispensable tools for acquiring vital information. The Property Intake educates your Property Manager on the detailed specifics of your home, covering aspects such as property features, unique characteristics, and any specific requirements. This information helps to market your property efficiently. The Owner Intake Form compiles comprehensive information about you, including contact details, emergency contacts, and any special preferences you may have. These forms are instrumental in fostering effective communication and ensuring that your Property Manager is well-informed about both the property itself and your specific needs, preferences, and desired level of involvement.

Additional Items:

Beyond the standard onboarding requirements, a reputable property management company takes a comprehensive approach, requesting owners to submit additional documents to enhance the efficiency and security of the property management process. This supplementary documentation includes:

- Valid Photo ID,
- Copy of Homeowner Association's Covenants, Conditions, and Restrictions CC&R's
- Mortgage information,
- Copy of the Rental Homeowners Insurance policy.

These documents serve critical roles, from identity verification to ensuring future tenants adhere to community guidelines outlined in the CC&R's. Moreover, they validate that owners are current on mortgage payments with sufficient insurance coverage. This meticulous documentation not only safeguards the interests of all parties involved but also fosters a transparent and responsible property management relationship.

W 9 Form:

The W9 Form is a component in adhering to IRS regulations and ensuring a streamlined financial reporting process. This procedural necessity requires owners to provide essential information, including their taxpayer identification number (TIN) or social security number. By completing the W9 Form, property managers and owners alike contribute to maintaining accurate records, promoting financial transparency, and upholding compliance with tax regulations.

ACH Direct Deposit Authorization Form:

Streamlining financial transactions is crucial for a hassle-free property management experience. The ACH Direct Deposit Authorization Form enables the property manager to efficiently disburse rent payments directly into the owner's designated bank account. The convenience offered by a property manager ensures a swift and secure financial flow, contributing to a smoother and more transparent property management relationship.

Authorization to Add Management as Additional Insured:

A reputable property management company typically requires being added to the property owner's insurance policy as an "Additional Insured" for liability purposes. This is an industry standard and is in the best interest of the property owner.

Authorization To Establish Utility Services:

This form grants the property manager the authority to establish and disconnect utility services on behalf of the owner. It also allows for the setup of utilities to automatically transfer payment responsibility to the owner when a tenant vacates the premises. This ensures that the property remains operational for showings, maintenance, and cleaning purposes.

Other Disclosure Examples: Various disclosure forms may be required:

- Mold Disclosure Waiver
- Lead-Based Paint disclosure
- Lock Box Addendum Disclosure
- Disclosures related to remodels or large-scale renovations

Plan to Bring your Home "Rent Ready"

Stay tuned for a deeper dive into the specifics of a "Rent Ready Home" focusing on the specific requirements.

What Does Rent Ready Mean?

Rent Ready

Understanding the concept of a "Rent Ready Home" extends beyond mere cleanliness and functionality; it scrutinizes the overall condition of the property. This comprehensive approach encompasses both interior and exterior repairs and upgrades, ensuring your property is safe, well-maintained, and meets minimum requirements. As a bonus, we'll provide you with a helpful checklist to ensure your property meets the "Rent Ready" criteria to ensure your property is ready for the rental market.

Whether you're a first-time landlord or seasoned in renting out properties, ensuring your property is rent-ready is paramount. Even if your property is in excellent condition or brand new, not all homes automatically meet the criteria for immediate rental readiness. To make your property rent-ready, you must take deliberate steps to ensure it is in optimal condition for the market.

Presenting a well-maintained, clean property serves dual purposes—it sets a high standard of care for potential applicants and positions you to command higher rents while minimizing the number of days your property sits vacant.

Rent Ready Standards

Rent Ready Condition means the condition in which the landlord or property manager delivers vacant units to new tenants, freshly painted and cleaned, with all appliances, fixtures, and equipment therein in good working order.

The following lists serve as a guideline to gauge what your property will need. Different property management companies have different minimums. However, this should serve as a realistic checklist to provide a clear picture of expectations. After your Property Manager performs the Onboarding Property Inspection, they will be able to provide you with a unique list of what needs to be done to bring your property rent-ready.

Standard Rent Ready Checklist:

- Smoke alarms must be in every bedroom and hallway in working condition, and not expired.
- Wiring inside and out must be to code; outlet covers, and switch covers must be installed.
- Carbon Monoxide Detectors and Fire Extinguisher must be installed on every level and not expired
- Door locks and window locks must operate easily; screens and screen should be free of holes.
- All light fixtures should have matching light LED bulbs.
- Doorstops should be installed or repaired for every door throughout the house.
- Sliding closet doors must be on tracks and slide easily.
- Fresh caulking should be applied around tubs and showers.

- Kitchen and bathroom fixtures should be free of leaks and drips.
- Toilets should flush easily and be free of any obstructions.
- All walls, ceilings, and baseboards should look fresh and clean, neutral in color.
- Nail holes should be filled, textured, and painted to blend with the rest of the walls.
- Flooring should be clean and in good repair; carpets should be free of stains and odors.
- Windows should be clean, and window coverings should be clean and fully operational.
- All appliances and systems are working as originally designed.
- The carpets have been professionally cleaned.
- New HVAC filters.
- Garage door opener and remotes function properly.
- Locks will be change or re-keyed after owner departs and between each tenant, at owner's expense
- Landscaping should be neat; bedding areas and lawns should be free of weeds.
- Trees and shrubs should be trimmed back.
- Fencing should be in good condition with adequate locking mechanisms.
- Sprinkler systems should be maintained and fully functioning.
- No missing shingles on the roof; gutters should be adequately attached and free of damage.
- Personal items or debris left behind should be removed.
- Oil or grease stains on driveways, walkways, or carports should be removed.

Rent Ready Cleaning Checklist:

Ensuring a professional level of cleanliness is imperative for vacant units brought under management. The following breakdown outlines the specific cleaning tasks expected in various areas of the property.

KITCHEN:

- Clean cabinets, drawers, and doors inside and out
- Clean microwave inside and out
- Range, hood, filter, and fan cleaning
- Clean oven inside, outside, and underneath
- Clean refrigerator inside, outside, and underneath
- Scrub sink, faucet, and countertops
- Vacuum and mop the floor
- Clean windows and window sills
- Dust and remove cobwebs
- Clean and dust lighting and other fixtures
- Wipe down baseboards

BATHROOMS:

- Clean shower, tub, and faucet
- Clean sink, countertops, and faucet
- Clean the toilet inside and outside
- Wipe down and clean cabinets and drawers inside and out
- Clean fixtures and towel bar
- Mop the floor
- Clean mirrors and any windows and window sills
- Wipe down baseboards

LIVING AREAS:

- Vacuum carpets and stairs
- Clean all windows and window sills
- Wipe down baseboards
- Mop entryways and other hard surface floors
- Dust and remove cobwebs
- Wipe down walls
- Clean fireplace
- Door knobs throughout the house
- Electrical outlets throughout the house
- Clean and dust blinds
- Wipe down lighting and fixtures
- Wipe down inside and outside of doors
- Clean the laundry area - top front, sides, inside, and under machines (if staying in home)

OUTSIDE AREAS:

- Clean and sweep front porch, patio areas, and outside/inside of all doors
- Ensure the lawn is freshly mowed, trimmed, and weeded. Remove any debris
- Clean out any storage areas, the interior of the garage, and sheds
- Clean all outside windows and lights by the front door, back door, patios, etc.

This comprehensive cleaning checklist ensures that your property is presented at the highest standard for potential tenants.

Property Managers are also Evaluating You and Your Property

Property management companies have minimum standards for the properties they are willing to represent. When talking with a property manager, remember, they're sizing you up too. If you're not on the same page about property standards, it might be a case of "It's not you, it's your property."

A piece of advice: Some property managers may pass on properties that need extensive work or owners unwilling to meet the rent-ready standard. This standard isn't for those looking to cut corners; it's tailored for owners committed to maintaining a high standard for their property.

Wait, there's more – property management companies come with their own set of rules. Some exclusively handle top-tier properties (Class "A" or "B"), while others welcome a broader range (including Class "C" & "D" properties). As you explore property management options, consider their preferences to ensure they align with your values and the type of property you own. It's about finding the right fit for your property and values.

Size Isn't Everything

Navigating the Myth of Property Management Companies

Welcome to this exclusive bonus chapter, where we debunk a common myth in the world of property management: the belief that the size of a management company is the ultimate indicator of its quality.

In the real estate landscape, it's easy to fall into the trap of assuming that bigger always means better or that smaller is synonymous with subpar service. However, this couldn't be further from the truth. Let's unravel the myth and gain a more distinctive perspective:

The Fallacy of Size

Small Doesn't Equal Bad:

- Personalized Attention
- Flexibility and Agility
- Community-Centric Focus

Big Doesn't Guarantee Excellence:

- Potential for Impersonal Service
- Bureaucratic Challenges
- Not Necessarily Local Experts

Assessing Quality Beyond Size

Client Testimonials and Reviews:

- Insights into Client Satisfaction
- Personal Experiences Matter

Services Tailored to Your Needs:

- Customization Trumps Size
- Your Property's Unique Requirements

Key Considerations When Choosing

Understanding Your Property's Needs:

- Size Compatibility
- Specialized vs. Generalized Management

Communication and Responsiveness:

- The Size-Agnostic Aspect
- Efficient Processes Over Company Size

Myth-Busting Success Stories

- Small Companies Delivering Exceptional Service
- Large Companies Embracing Personalized Approaches

The Middle Ground

Medium-Sized Companies:

- Balancing Act Between Personalization and Resources
- Often Overlooked Gems in Property Management

In conclusion, it's crucial to approach the selection of a property management company with an open mind. Size is just one variable in the equation, and the key lies in finding the right fit for your unique needs. So, whether big or small, what matters most is the company's dedication, expertise, and commitment to your property's success.

As we navigate the myths together, remember: "A small-sized property management company does not represent it's bad, nor does a large-sized property management mean they are good." The perfect fit is about aligning with a company that understands and values your investment as much as you do.

Making the Final Decision

As we conclude our journey of how to hire a great property manager, we find ourselves at the pivotal moment of making the final decision. Throughout this book, we've explored the fundamental aspects that contribute to a successful partnership with a property manager. Now, let's distill the key takeaways that should guide your decision-making process.

Emphasizing Quality

Quality stands as the cornerstone of a fruitful collaboration with a property manager. From the initial evaluation of your property to the ongoing management tasks, insist on a commitment to excellence. Seek out a property manager who not only meets the industry standards but exceeds them. Quality management ensures that your property is well-maintained, attracts reliable tenants, and operates efficiently. Don't compromise on quality, for it forms the bedrock of a successful property management relationship.

Asking the right Questions

Asking the right questions is not just about gathering information; it's about sculpting a comprehensive understanding of how your property manager operates. Armed with these inquiries, you're poised to make a well-informed decision that aligns with your property management aspirations. May your choice be astute and may your property flourish under the guidance of an exceptional property manager.

Understanding is Key

Throughout this book, we've underscored the significance of clear communication and a shared understanding between you and your property manager. The ability to comprehend each other's expectations, responsibilities, and goals is vital for a harmonious partnership. A property manager who takes the time to understand your unique preferences, concerns, and long-term objectives is an invaluable asset. Look for a manager who prioritizes open and transparent communication, fostering an environment of mutual understanding.

Value-driven Approach

Value transcends mere monetary considerations. In the realm of property management, it involves the worth a manager adds to your investment beyond the financial aspect. Evaluate potential property managers based on the value they bring to the table. This includes their proficiency in maximizing rental income, minimizing vacancies, and navigating legal and maintenance challenges. A property manager who adds substantial value ensures a solid return on your investment and contributes to the overall success of your real estate venture.

Making the Final Decision

As we navigate towards the crucial juncture of making the final decision, it's imperative to meticulously assess the quality, understanding, and value each potential property manager brings to the table. Drawing from the wisdom imparted in this book, reflect on the key takeaways and the insightful questions you've asked throughout the selection process.

Consider how each candidate aligns with your expectations and property management objectives. Dive into references and reviews, scrutinize their track record, and, significantly, continue to pose the right questions during the interview process. Trust your instincts; opt for a property manager whose qualifications not only align on paper but also resonate with your overarching vision for your property.

Keep in mind, the decision-making phase is more than just a financial transaction. It's about selecting a property manager who embodies your property management goals and shares a vision for the success of your investment.

Additional Resources

The journey doesn't end with the hiring process; it's an ongoing collaboration. To support you in navigating the dynamic landscape of property management, we recommend exploring additional resources. Stay informed with industry publications and engage with online forums to exchange insights with fellow property owners and property management groups. Leverage online platforms, webinars, and podcasts dedicated to real estate and property management for continuous learning.

Conclusion: Hiring a Great Property Manager

Discover the Best Questions to Ask Before Hiring a Property Manager

I n conclusion, making the final property management selection involves a comprehensive evaluation of quality, understanding, and value. Asking the right questions will help choose a property manager who aligns with your objectives and exhibits a commitment to excellence. Arm yourself with ongoing resources and support to navigate the ever-evolving landscape of property management.

May your partnership with a property manager be prosperous, fulfilling, and built on a foundation of mutual success.

If you found this book helpful, we would greatly appreciate an honest and thoughtful review. Your feedback is valuable to us and helps others discover the benefits of this resource.

Thank you for taking the time to share your thoughts.

Resources

R obert Kiyosaki. (2015). *Rich Dad Poor Dad: What The Rich Teach Their Kids About Money That the Poor and Middle Class Do Not!*, p.179. Robert Kiyosaki.

OpenAI. (2022). *ChatGPT Language Model*. OpenAI. https://platform.o penai.com/models/chatgpt

NARPM. (n.d.). *About NARPM® - National Association of Residential Property Managers*. National Association of Residential Property Managers. https://www.narpm.org/about/

Laura. (2023a, December 22). *ZInspector – Property Inspection Solutions (Mobile & Office)*. zInspector. https://www.zinspector.com/

HUD, ADA, FHACT - PetScreening. (n.d.). https://www.petscreening. com/resources/hud-ada-fhact-links

Assistance Animals - PetScreening. (n.d.). https://www.petscreening.co m/solutions/assistance-animals

www.ingramcontent.com/pod-product-compliance
Lightning Source LLC
Chambersburg PA
CBHW070818290526
45795CB00002B/755